What Animals Live in the DESERT?

Animal Book 4-6 Years Old
Children's Animal Books

BABY PROFESSOR
EDUCATION KIDS

Speedy Publishing LLC
40 E. Main St. #1156
Newark, DE 19711
www.speedypublishing.com

Animals and insects that are able to survive in the desert include, but are not limited to, the **Camel, Meerkat, Scorpions** and **Grasshoppers.** In this book, you will learn about these animals and how they are able to survive the heat and dryness of the desert climate.

How Do Animals Survive in the Desert?

They adapt for survival in spite of its lack of water and its extreme temperatures. Many sleep during the day when it is very hot and come out when it is cooler at night (this is known as nocturnal). They sleep in tunnels under the ground, known as burrows, during the day so they can remain cool.

These animals need very little water and get most of their needed water from their food. Some animals have the ability to store the water to use at a later time. Let's learn about some of these amazing animals of the desert!

Wild Camels

Bactrian Camel

What Does the Bactrian Camel Look Like?

This camel is most known for the two huge humps located on its back. It can grow to be more than seven feet tall at its shoulder! It grows to be more than eleven feet long and can weigh more than 2000 pounds (that's more than a ton)! Its brown fur coat keeps it warm in the winter by growing shaggy and long and then sheds for the heat of the summer.

What Do They Eat?

They eat plants, which means they are known as herbivores. They are able to eat almost all types of vegetation including thorny, bitter or dry plants that are not eaten by other animals. They have a tough digestive system and have even been known to eat clothing, shoes and even dead carcasses.

Bactrian Camel portrait close up in Himalayas.

Where Do They Live?

They live in the Taklamaken and Gobi deserts which are located in north central Asia.

Bactrian Camel in the desert

Do They Travel in Packs?

They tend to travel in packs of 6 to 20. On occasion, they may gather near waters sources in larger groups.

Bactrian Camels

What About Their Humps?

Camels have the ability to store fat in the humps on their back. This fat can then be converted to energy and water when they haven't had access to water or food for a long time. The humps become floppy and thin once they have utilized the fat.

Bactrian Camel

The Bactrian Camels can go for month without water because of the energy stored in their humps. However, when a camel is thirsty it can drink more than 30 gallons of water in just a few minutes.

Bactrian Camel in Hunder Sand Dunes of Nubra Valley

What Makes Them an Ideal Animal for the Desert?

In addition to having the humps so that they can go without water for a long period of time, they have other ways to survive the desert. Their long eyelashes and bushy eyebrows shield their eyes from the desert sand.

Their nostrils are able to close to keep the sand out of their nose. In addition, they have tough, big footpads helping them to carry heavy containers over the tough terrain of the desert. These assets make them a great animal to carry travelers through the desert.

Are They Endangered?

The Bactrian Camels are considered to be critically endangered. This indicates they are close to being extinct. While the population of this camel is on the decline, it is thought that there are approximately 600 that live in the wild. In the Gobi Desert there are two preserves helping protect this species, one located in Mongolia and one located in China.

Bactrian Camel in desert of Nubra Valley, Ladakh, North India

Meerkat (Surikate)

Meerkat

The Meerkat is a small mammal and is a part of the family known as the mongoose. They became famous from the television show Meerkat Manor on the Animal Planet station. This TV show followed many families of Meerkats located in the Kalahari Desert. Its scientific name is suricata surricatta.

Where Do They Live?

They live in the Kalahari Desert located in South Africa and Botswana. They are able to dig great networks of tunnels underground and this is where they live during the night. The tunnels have several openings if they need to escape a predator.

Two Meerkats in Botswana

Do Meerkats Live in a Group?

Meerkats live in family groups known as gangs, mobs, or clans. The amount of meerkats in a gang varies. Typically the number is approximately 20 members however, they can grow to have 50 members. They work together to assist each other. One or two will be on the lookout for predators as the others hunt for food. If a predator is spotted, the lookouts will let out a warning bark and the remaining family will escape into its underground burrow.

Each clan will have an alpha pair that will lead the group. This pair will typically have the right for mating and producing offspring. If the other members of a gang reproduce, the alpha pair will typically kill the offspring and kick its mother out of the gang.

Their Territory

Each clan has a territory and they mark it with their scent. It is typically an area of about four square miles. They will not allow any other groups of meerkats in their territory and they will fight, if necessary. They move through their territory each day attempting to find food in different areas.

Group Meerkats

What Do They Eat?

They eat both animals and plants, which makes them omnivores. While they eat mostly insects, they also eat fruit, eggs, snakes and lizards. They are also able to eat poisonous prey such as scorpions since their bodies are resistant to their poison. In order to maintain their energy, they have to eat every day since their bodies do not have the ability to store much fat.

Group Hug - Meerkats huddled together on a rainy day because of the cold.

Why Do They Stand Up So Straight?

Typically, the lookout, known as the sentry, will use its tail for balance and stand up on its hind legs. They do this to look for predators.

Family of Meerkats

Two Scorpions

Scorpions

What Is A Scorpion?

Scorpions are classified as arachnids, not an insect. They are similar to a spider in that they have eight legs. The Emperor and the Arizona Bark scorpions are only two of the over 1700 species of scorpions. They are all different, but their features are similar.

What Do They Look Like?

While they have eight legs, similar to the other arachnids, they also have two large pinchers and a long tail with a venomous stinger. The exoskeleton on the outside is a hard shell which varies in color, including black, brown, blue, green, and yellow. Their length ranges from one inch to more than eight inches long.

Striped Bark Scorpion

Where Do They Live?

Scorpions live almost anywhere, including rainforests, caves, grasslands, and deserts. They will burrow in the ground in sand, rocks, or soil so that they cannot be found by predators and prey.

Striped Bark Scorpion

What Do They Like To Eat?

Scorpions mostly eat insects, but the larger ones might eat a lizard or a small rodent. As they hunt, they use their claws and paralyze their prey with the stinger.

Scorpion eating grasshopper

How Poisonous are They?

They are all considered poisonous. Some are specific for a certain prey and are more toxic to the different animals. About 25 species are lethal to humans, so you do not want to play with one of them. If you see one, let your teacher or parents known immediately.

Closeup view of a Scorpion in nature.

Are They Considered To Be Endangered?

Some are rarer than other, but they are not endangered. The Emperor, and some other species are considered to be protected so that they cannot be removed from their habitat.

Bark Scorpion - Centruroides Exilicauda (formerly C. Sculpturatus)

Grasshopper

Grasshoppers

The term Grasshopper is used to describe several insects falling under a scientific "suborder" Caelifera, in the order of the Orthoptera. There are more than 11,000 species in this suborder.

The grasshopper has six legs, a head, a thorax and an abdomen, similar to other insects. In addition, it has a hard outer shell, known as an exoskeleton, which protects the soft insides of the grasshopper. They also have two pairs of wings, the back wings are larger than the front wings and the front wings are fairly hard and small. They have large back legs which helps them to jump.

Typically, they are brown, but other colors include reddish brown, yellowish brown and light green and some are striped.

Grasshoppers can be found all over the world, other than areas where it is too cold, such as the south and north poles. They adapt to about all habitats including grasslands, forests, and deserts.

Grasshopper sitting on a rock

What Do They Eat?

They typically will feed on plants, primarily grasses, leaves and cereal crops. Many eat a lot of food, including crops of farmers, creating serious problems for the farmers.

Now that you have learned about a few of the animals of the desert, you can do your own research to find out what other animals can survive in the desert by going to the local library, researching the internet or asking questions of your teachers, family and friends.

Visit

BABY PROFESSOR
EDUCATION KIDS

www.BabyProfessorBooks.com

to download Free Baby Professor eBooks
and view our catalog of new and exciting
Children's Books

Made in the USA
San Bernardino, CA
30 April 2019